Doris Kutschbach

The Art Treasure Hunt

I Spy with My Little Eye

PRESTEL   Munich · London · New York

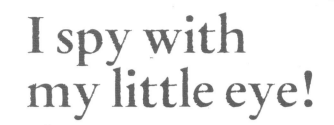

I spy with my little eye!

There's a lot to discover in this big art book.

Let's play!

I spy ...

- a rocking horse,

- an animal with
  a checkered rear end,

- a turtle with
  a light-blue shell,

- a light-blue jellyfish with
  colored tentacles.

Do you see them too?

Can you also find the three creatures
above and below in the big painting?

What are the people doing in the palace park?

Can you find a tower clock, two dogs playing together, a peacock sitting on a wall? Where is the woman climbing into a boat?

What else can you discover?

Do you like being at the lake?

Can you spot a sailboat and a little monkey?
And where is the man playing music?
What are the other people doing?

Come join everyone in the garden!

I spy ...

a great maharaja,
two elephants,
three golden bowls,
two peacocks,
a pool of water,
and several birdcages.

Can you **find all of these things,** as well as the **details** above and below, **in the big painting?**

Pointed and round, a riot of colors!

I spy with my little eye: something ...

- **bright blue**
- bright yellow
- dark yellow
- **brown**
- **red**
- light green
- pink

- gray
- light blue
- **dark green**
- **black**
- white
- orange
- **purple**

- **angular**
- **round**
- **long**
- **pointed**
- **thick**
- **thin**
- **triangular**

- **rectangular**
- **circular**
- **diamond-shaped**
- **oval-shaped**

Try to find ...

- **two dogs**
- **a factory**
- **a boy with red hair and a pointed cap**
- **two men with vendor's trays**

There was a fisherman named Fisher who fished for some fish in a fissure.

Which of these animals live entirely in water?

Can you find these details in the big picture?

I spy
with my little eye...

Let's play too!

The children are at home.

Can you find these details in the big picture?

Brrrr, it's cold!

In winter you can go ice skating, play ice hockey, and run across a frozen lake. What do you like to do in winter?

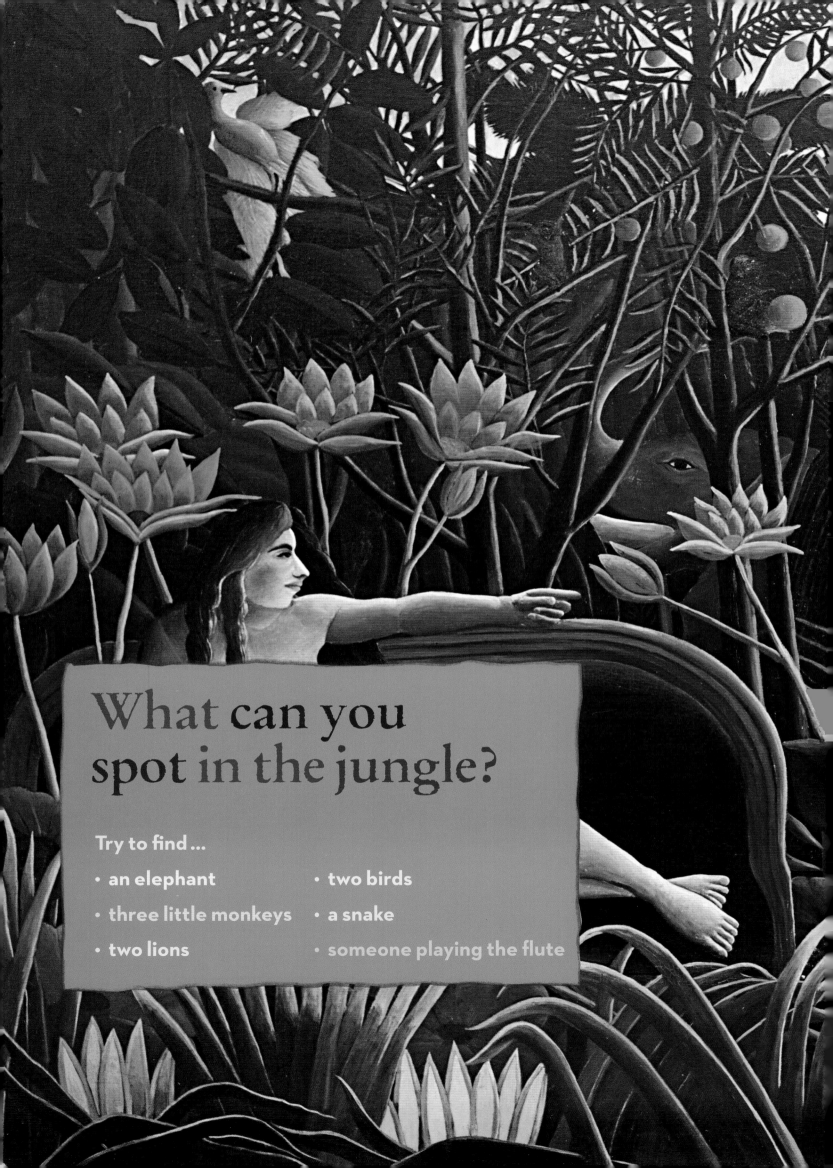

What can you spot in the jungle?

Try to find ...

- **an elephant**
- **three little monkeys**
- **two lions**
- **two birds**
- **a snake**
- **someone playing the flute**

- **two tight-rope walkers above the palace garden**
- **a group of musicians**
- a girl in a yellow dress
- **a fountain**
- a woman holding her head in suspense
- **the details below**

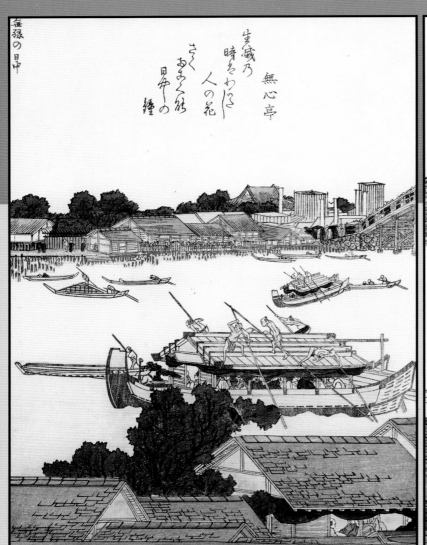

There's lots of activity on the river.

Many of the boats are covered with roofs.
Can you find someone all alone in a boat?
Can you find the boatsmen standing on the roof?

So many people are crowded on the bridge.

Can you also find the red flag, three light-blue umbrellas, an old man with a polka-dot robe, and three ladies with elegant, pinned-up hairdos?

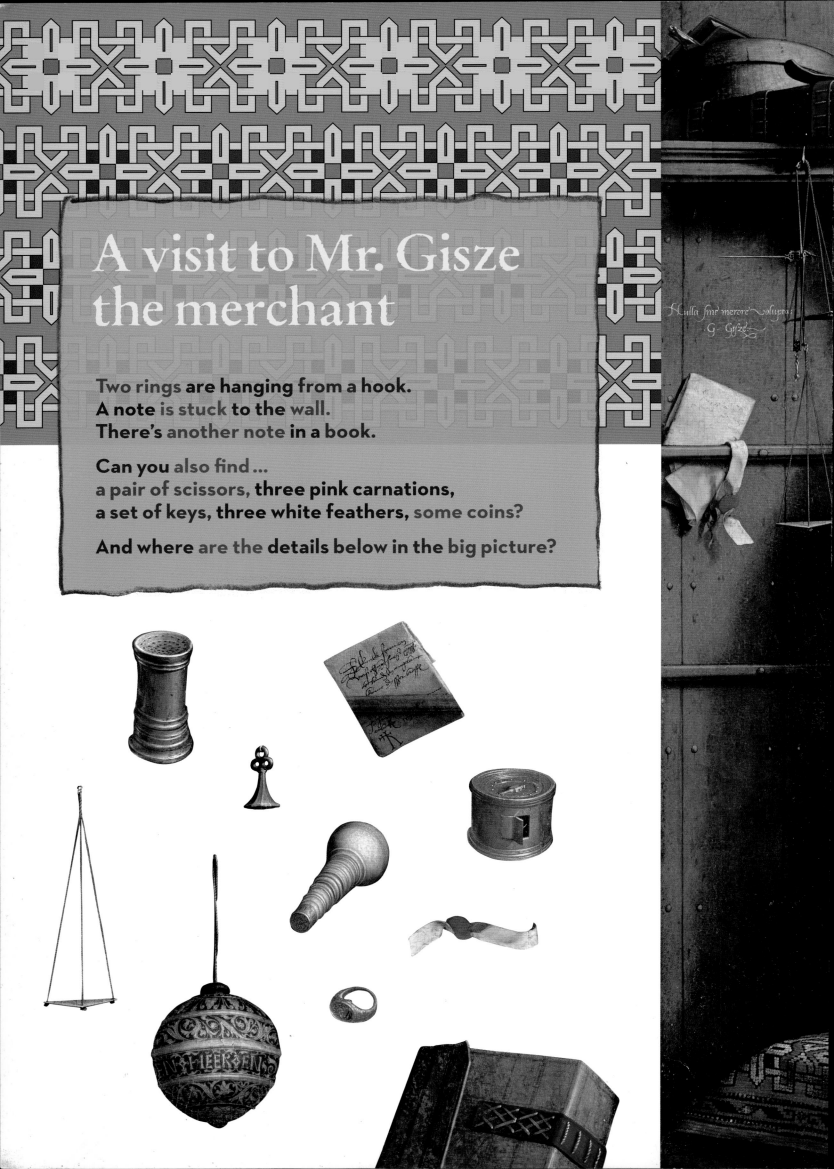

A visit to Mr. Gisze the merchant

Two rings **are hanging from a hook.**
A note is stuck **to the** wall.
There's another note in a book.

Can you also find ...
a pair of scissors, **three pink carnations,**
a set of keys, three white feathers, some coins?

And where are the **details below in the big picture?**

A visit to Mr. Adam the painter

Can you find a picture of the white horse? And a sculpture? Can you find a drawing of the dog that's lying on the floor? What do you think Mr. Adam the painter (in the black cap) is painting? Which animal would you like to paint best? Can you also find the horse's saddle, three bottles, a lady's hat, a mare with her foal, and a dog's collar?

This is the way the ladies ride...

There are **horses** **hiding** in this picture. Do you see them?

Can you find these details in the big picture?

Look: two red dogs are dancing!

Can you also see the man who's standing on his head and the four crawling babies? What else can you find?

Some of the forms in this picture have been copied above. Can you find them below?

Good night!

Do you see the deer? And the two Indians hunting him?
Can you find these other details in the big painting?

There are six birdcages in the upper half of the picture. Another cage is probably represented in the middle row.

The Pictures in This Book

1 *Wassily Kandinsky*
Sky Blue (1940)

Oil on canvas, 100 × 73 cm · Paris, Centre Pompidou.
Photo: bpk | CNAC-MNAM | Philippe Migeat

The painter Wassily Kandinsky lived from 1866 to 1944. His early paintings showed many motifs from his Russian homeland, but these objects later began to disappear from his increasingly abstract pictures.

2 *Hans Bol*
Park Landscape with Castle (1589)

Body color on parchment, 23,5 × 32,5 cm · Old Master Paintings, Berlin State Museums. Photo: bpk | Jörg P. Anders

Hans Bol (1534–1593) came from a Flemish family of painters and worked during the periods of art history called the High Renaissance and Mannerism. He painted primarily landscapes, Biblical and mythological scenes, and scenes of everyday life.

3 *Georges Seurat*
A Sunday Afternoon on the Island of La Grande Jatte (1884–1886)

Oil on canvas, 207,5 × 308 cm · Chicago, Art Institute.
Photo: Artothek | Joseph S. Martin

The French painter Georges Seurat (1859–1891) was a great fan of artists called the Impressionists. Like them, he studied how the human eye perceives color. He invented the technique of pointillism, in which the paint is placed on the canvas in small dots. The viewer's eye then mixes the dots together to perceive the image's forms and colors.

4 **Maharaja at a Garden Concert**
Indian miniature (early 18th c.)

Body color on paper, 47 × 61,5 cm · Museum of Asian Art, Berlin State Museums. Photo: bpk | Iris Papadopoulos

An unknown artist from the city of Sarwar in the Indian state of Rajasthan painted this picture. The painting, which features an Indian prince called a maharaja, was created there in the eighteenth century.

5 *Kazimir Malevich*
Suprematism (Supremus No. 56, 1916)

Oil on canvas, 80,5 × 71 cm · St. Petersburg, The Russian Museum. Photo: bpk | Roman Beniaminson

In 1915 the Russian artist Kazimir Malevich (1878–1935) developed a style he called "Suprematism." He sought to create a perfectly abstract art. His Suprematist pictures, like this one, are composed only of simple geometric shapes.

Solution to picture 9

Robert Delaunay
The Joy of Life (1930)

Oil on canvas, 200 × 228 cm · Paris, Centre Pompidou.
Photo: bpk | Paris, Centre Pompidou | Philippe Migeat

The French artist Robert Delaunay (1885–1941) is one of the most important modern artists. He and his wife Sonia helped found the artistic movement called Orphism, in which predominantly round forms are created in strong, bright colors.

L.S. Lowry
Good Friday, Daisy Nook (1946)

Oil on canvas, 76 × 102 cm · private collection. Photo: Corbis

The English artist Lawrence Stephen Lowry (1887–1976), known as L. S. Lowry, painted primarily scenes of life in the industrial regions of northern England. His pictures are typically inhabited by a multitude of small figures, or "matchstick men."

Fishing on the Nile
Ancient Egyptian Wall Painting (12th Dynasty)

Lithograph. Photo: bpk

The flattened representation of figures and objects in this painting is typical of Egyptian art. There is no perspective, no use of diagonal viewpoints, and no overlapping. Everything is arranged next to and above everything else. Many Egyptian wall paintings were found in graves, and they were meant to remind the souls of the dead of life on Earth.

Balthasar van der Ast
Still Life with Basket of Fruits (1632)

Oil on oak panel, 14,5 × 20 cm · Gemäldegalerie, Berlin State Museums. Photo: bpk | Jörg P. Anders

Balthasar van der Ast was born in the Netherlands in 1593 or 1594 and died in Delft in 1657. He specialized in still lifes. Like so many images from the Baroque period of art, this van der Ast painting shows insects and contains hints of the perishability of the fruits. It is thus also a reminder of the transience of life.

Giuseppe Arcimboldo
Spring (1573)

Oil on canvas, 76 × 64 cm · Paris, Musée du Louvre. Photo: Artothek

The Italian artist Giuseppe Arcimboldo (ca. 1526–1593) was the court painter for Emperor Rudolph II in Prague, which is now in the Czech Republic. His pictures are characteristic of the quirky, often humorous art of Mannerism. He composed a portrait of a librarian out of books and painted the seasons in the form of heads made of flowers and fruits.

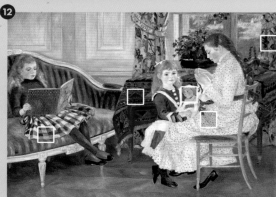

⑪ *Pieter Bruegel the Elder*
Children's Games (1560)

Oil on oak panel, 118 × 161 cm · Vienna, Kunsthistorisches Museum.
Photo: bpk | Hermann Buresch

Many of the games shown here are still known.
The Netherlandish artist Pieter Bruegel the
Elder (1528–1569) painted predominantly
scenes of everyday peasant life, earning him the
nickname "Peasant Bruegel." His pictures often
contain deeper meanings: they sometimes refer
to proverbs, for example, or hint at human folly.

⑫ *Pierre-Auguste Renoir*
Children's Afternoon in Wargemont (1884)

Oil on canvas, 127 × 173 cm · Nationalgalerie, Berlin State
Museums. Photo: bpk | Jörg P. Anders

The French painter Pierre-Auguste Renoir
(1841–1919) joined the Impressionists, who were
not taken seriously by the public for a long time.
Since he enjoyed painting social events, he later
received many commissions for portraits of
wealthy patrons, with which he was able to make
a living.

⑬ *Hendrick Avercamp*
Ice Landscape (first half of the 17th c.)

Oil on wood panel, 67,5 × 115 cm · Staatliches Museum Schwerin,
Photo: bpk | Staatliches Museum Schwerin | Dirk Dunkelberg

Dutch artist Hendrick Avercamp (1585–1634)
lived in Amsterdam and Kampen. He was deaf
and never learned to speak. It was said that as a
child he often went ice skating with his parents.
Perhaps this explains the delightful winter
landscapes he later painted, with their richly
detailed depictions of popular culture.

⑭ *Henri Rousseau*
The Dream (1910)

Oil on canvas, 205 × 299 cm · New York, Museum of Modern Art.
Photo: Artothek

The French artist Henri Rousseau (1844–1910)
was a customs officer who taught himself painting, which was his hobby as well as his passion.
He never travelled; the many exotic plants in his
famous images of the jungle were inspired by
plants from the botanical garden in Paris.

⑮ **Tight-Rope Walkers**
Indian miniature (ca. 1785)

Body color and gold on paper · Museum of Asian Art, Berlin State
Museums. Photo: bpk | Jürgen Liepe

This precious painting with body color and gold
comes from India. The tightrope walkers above
the magnificent palace are depicted with fine
brushstrokes in great detail.

⑯ *Hokusai*
**People on the Ryōgoku Bridge and
Boots on the Sumida** (ca. 1803)

Woodcut · Leiden, Nationalmuseum für Völkerkunde, Photo:
Nationalmuseum für Völkerkunde, Leiden

The colored woodcuts of the Japanese master
Katsushika Hokusai (1760–1849) are among the
most important works of Japanese art. Already
in the nineteenth century they were coveted
collectors' items in Europe, and Impressionist
artists were greatly inspired by them.

Solution: The tall boy to the left (behind Mr. Adam) is probably portraying the man on the far left side of the stage. The painter Mr. Adam is painting the white horse and the man standing next to the horses.

17 *Hans Holbein the Younger*
Portrait of Georg Gisze (1532)

Oil on oak panel, 97,5 × 86 cm · Gemäldegalerie, Staatliche Museen zu Berlin. Photo: bpk | Jörg P. Anders

Hans Holbein the Younger was born in Augsburg in 1497 or 1498 and died in 1543 in London. He was one of the most important early Renaissance painters in Germany. Even today we are still fascinated by the incredibly detailed naturalism of every single object in his paintings.

18 *Albrecht Adam*
The Artist's Studio in Munich (1835)

Oil on oak panel, 62,5 × 84 cm · Nationalgalerie, Berlin State Museums. Photo: bpk | Andres Kilger

The German painter Albrecht Adam (1786–1862) is known above all for battle scenes and portraits. This picture offers an interesting view into a painter's studio in the nineteenth century.

19 *Franz Marc*
Stables (1913)

Oil on canvas, 74 × 157,5 cm · New York, Solomon R. Guggenheim Museum. Photo: Artothek | Blauel/Gnamm

Franz Marc was born in 1880 in Munich. There he got to know Wassily Kandinsky, and together they founded the artist's group the Blaue Reiter, or Blue Rider. Marc nearly always painted animals, which he felt closer to than people. He died a young man in 1916, during the First World War.

20 *Keith Haring*
Untitled (1981)

Ink stick and acrylic paint on paper, 272 × 472,5 cm · Greenwich, Brant Foundation, Photo: The Keith Haring Foundation

The American artist Keith Haring (1958–1990) died much too young: in New York City at the age of thirty-two of AIDS. His works recall graffiti and comics; he brought art to the streets and spoke to a young generation. His expressive artistic language of signs and symbols is understandable to everyone.

21 *Henry Lewis*
Indians Hunting Deer at Night on the Mississippi (1863)

Oil on canvas, 32 × 51 cm · private collection, Photo: Artothek | Bayer & Mitko

In 1836 the English painter Henry Lewis (1819–1904) arrived in St. Louis in the USA, where he began his career as a landscape painter. In 1848 he painted a giant panorama of the Mississippi, with which he toured through large cities in the USA, Canada, and Europe.

© Prestel Verlag, Munich · London · New York, 2012
© for the works held by the artists or their legal heirs
except for: Wassily Kandinsky and L.S. Lowry:
VG Bild-Kunst, Bonn 2012; Keith Haring: The Keith Haring
Foundation 2012.

Library of Congress Control Number: 2011942236; British
Library Cataloguing-in-Publication Data: a catalogue record
for this book is available from the British Library; Deutsche
Nationalbibliothek holds a record of this publication in the
Deutsche Nationalbibliografie; detailed bibliographical data
can be found under: http://dnb.ddb.de

Front cover: Henri Rousseau: The Dream (detail)
Back cover: Hans Bol: Park Landscape with Castle (detail)

Prestel, a member of Verlagsgruppe Random House GmbH

Prestel Verlag, Munich
www.prestel.de

Prestel Publishing Ltd.
4 Bloomsbury Place
London WC1A 2QA

Prestel Publishing
900 Broadway, Suite 603
New York, NY 10003

www.prestel.com

Prestel books are available worldwide. Please contact
your nearest bookseller or one of the above addresses for
information concerning your local distributor.

Text and image selection: Doris Kutschbach
Translation: Cynthia Hall
Editor: Brad Finger
Design, layout and typesetting:
SOFAROBOTNIK, Augsburg & Munich
Production: Nele Krüger
Art Direction: Cilly Klotz
Origination: Reproline Mediateam, Munich
Printing and Binding: Tien Wah, Malaysia

FSC
www.fsc.org

MIX
Paper from
responsible sources
FSC® C012700

Verlagsgruppe Random House FSC-DEU-0100
The FSC-certified paper *HannoArt Silk* is produced by mill
Sappi, Alfeld.

ISBN 978-3-7913-7097-2